Praise for P.K. Subban

"An excellent book with an important message, especially for young players of minorities who are trying to break into professional hockey. Work hard and stay dedicated."

— Carl Weekes, father of former
NHL goaltender Kevin Weekes

"A wonderful record of a talented and determined young Canadian who reached for his goals and an amazing family that has been with him every step of the way."

— Gord Simmonds, former owner and
league governor, Belleville Bulls

P.K. Subban

Fighting racism to become a hockey superstar and a role model for athletes of colour

Catherine Rondina

James Lorimer & Company Ltd., Publishers
Toronto

James Lorimer & Company Ltd., Publishers acknowledges funding support from the Ontario Arts Council (OAC), an agency of the Government of Ontario. We acknowledge the support of the Canada Council for the Arts, which last year invested $153 million to bring the arts to Canadians throughout the country. This project has been made possible in part by the Government of Canada and with the support of Ontario Creates.

Cover design: Gwen North
Cover images: Alamy and Aaron Bell

Library and Archives Canada Cataloguing in Publication

Title: P.K. Subban : fighting racism to become a hockey superstar and role model for athletes of colour / Catherine Rondina
Names: Rondina, Catherine, author.
Series: Recordbooks.
Description: Series statement: Recordbooks | Includes index.
Identifiers: Canadiana (print) 20190190043 | Canadiana (ebook) 20190190051 | ISBN 9781459415089 (softcover) | ISBN 9781459415096 (EPUB)
Subjects: LCSH: Subban, P. K., 1989- —Juvenile literature. | LCSH: Hockey players—Canada—Biography— Juvenile literature. | CSH: Black Canadian hockey players—Canada—Biography—Juvenile literature| LCGFT: Biographies.
Classification: LCC GV848.5.S92 R66 2020 | DDC j796.962092—dc23

Published by:
James Lorimer &
Company Ltd., Publishers
117 Peter Street, Suite 304
Toronto, ON, Canada
M5V 0M3
www.lorimer.ca

Distributed in Canada by:
Formac Lorimer Books
5502 Atlantic Street
Halifax, NS, Canada
B3H 1G4

Distributed in the US by:
Lerner Publisher Services
1251 Washington Ave. N.
Minneapolis, MN, USA
55401
www.lernerbooks.com

Printed and bound in Canada.
Manufactured by Marquis in Montmagny, Quebec in January 2020.
Job #181225

For those who stand up

Develop enough courage
so that you can stand up
for yourself
and then stand up
for somebody else.
— Maya Angelou

In Memory of J.M.

Contents

Prologue
Playing Through the Hurt

It's playoff season, a hockey fan's favourite time of the year!

On May 1, 2014, the Montreal Canadiens are facing the Boston Bruins in the second round of the playoffs for the **Stanley Cup**. Tensions are high between these two teams. Their history goes all the way back to the start of the National Hockey League (NHL), as both of them are Original Six teams. They have clashed on the ice since pro hockey's start.

Game 1 of the series is at the TD Garden arena in Boston, in front of a sellout crowd of 17,565 fans. P.K. Subban is a young, black **defenceman** on the Montreal team, proud and excited to be playing. All he can hear is the sound of his own heart pounding in his chest.

The game has been close and hard-fought. P.K. scored the first goal of the game in the first period. But Montreal lost a 2–0 lead in the second, and the teams have been trading goals ever since. The players on both ends of the ice are frustrated as the horn sounds to end the third period with the game tied 3–3. The game is going to sudden-death **overtime**, where the first team to score wins.

The players hit the ice and wait for the other team to make the one mistake that might lead to the winning goal. But after 20 minutes of overtime the game still remains tied.

As the teams get ready for the second overtime, they have already played more than 80 minutes of hockey. It's time for a hero to step up. That's when P.K. Subban sees his chance, an open line to the Boston net. P.K. lifts his stick in the air and shoots a **slapshot** from the blue line. His eyes follow the small black disc as it thunders toward the net. At 4:17 of the second overtime period, P.K.'s shot whisks past the glove of Boston goaltender Tuukka Rask. P.K. has scored the winning overtime goal for Montreal!

The Montreal Canadiens are all smiles as they congratulate each other on the win. P.K. has been on the ice for this game longer than any other player, with 33 minutes and 49 seconds of ice time. He was the hottest player on the rink. The big, bright smile on his face says it all. But Boston fans are not impressed. They throw their garbage and giveaway towels on the ice as the players skate off. Upset, they boo the Canadiens.

It is what happens after the teams leave the rink that shocks hockey fans everywhere. Within minutes of P.K.'s game-winning goal, hateful tweets begin to be posted on Twitter. Racist hockey fans, some even using the **hashtag** N-word, lash out at P.K. Subban. They tweet cruel, hurtful comments about Montreal's star of the game. They call P.K. names, using insults that attack him as a person of colour.

With the incredible overtime goal still in his head, P.K. tries to keep the win in focus. He played a key role in the game. He is proud of what he did on the ice. It was an important night for him and his Montreal teammates. But sadly, P.K. realizes that the ugliness of racism has become the focus of the game once again.

1 It's Hockey Night in Canada!

Every NHL family has a story to tell. For the Subban family, the story is unlike any other in the National Hockey League. P.K. is a talented black athlete whose family simply fell in love with Canada's game. Unlike most hockey stories, this one didn't begin in the land of ice and snow. It began on two small islands in the sun-filled Caribbean ocean.

In 1970, P.K.'s father, Karl, moved to Canada with his parents from Jamaica

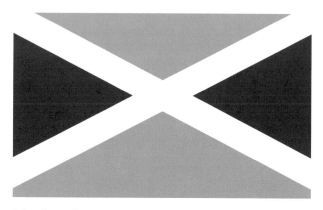

The flag of Jamaica.

when he was 11 years old. P.K.'s mother, Maria, arrived in Toronto, Ontario the same year with her family from Montserrat. Karl's family lived in the northern Ontario town of Sudbury. They were the only black family in their neighbourhood. It was mostly a French-speaking community and young Karl didn't know the language. But that didn't stop him from watching the most popular thing on TV on Saturday, *Hockey Night in Canada*. The game was broadcast in French and Karl didn't know what the announcers were saying, but it didn't matter. He loved the game! Most of the people in Sudbury were Montreal Canadiens fans, and Karl cheered right along with them. He began to play road hockey and eventually got a used pair of skates to play ice hockey with the boys in his neighbourhood. Karl quickly took the goaltender position for his team, just like he was goalkeeper when he had played soccer back in Jamaica. He often pretended that he was Ken Dryden, the star goalie for the Canadiens. Many years later, Karl would realize how hockey made him feel he belonged. Even though the kids he played with didn't speak the same language as him, sports could some-how bring them together.

As a teenager, Karl played a lot of sports. He was a natural athlete at Sudbury Secondary School. Basketball had become his new passion and he was good at it. Karl took his love of sports with him when he attended Lakehead University in Thunder

Bay, Ontario. There, he played basketball and dreamed of becoming an NBA player one day. But by the time Karl graduated from university, he had found his true passion. He was going to be a teacher. He studied hard and earned a teaching degree.

It was when Karl moved to Toronto that he met and eventually married Maria. One of the things they shared was a love of hockey. Maria had grown up in Toronto and had played a number of sports too. As a young girl, she was a provincial champion sprinter. Maria was also a diehard Toronto Maple Leafs fan, while Karl was still cheering for

Original Six

When the NHL was founded in 1917, there were six teams. Called the Original Six, the teams were the Montreal Canadiens, the Toronto Maple Leafs, the Detroit Red Wings, the Chicago Blackhawks, the Boston Bruins and the New York Rangers. All six of these teams are still part of the NHL today!

Hockey Night in Canada

In 1952, when the CBC started broadcasting in Canada, *Hockey Night in Canada* was on the air! Announcer Foster Hewitt started the show with the now famous words, "Hello, Canada and hockey fans in the United States and Newfoundland." The first game was between the Toronto Maple Leafs and the Boston Bruins.

his favourite boyhood team, the Montreal Canadiens. There has always been a huge rivalry between these two Original Six teams, and Karl and Maria kept that competition going strong. When they watched the two teams play against each other on TV, the Subban household could get pretty loud!

Karl and Maria were eager to have a family together. They had two daughters, three years apart, named Nastassia and Natasha. On May 13, 1989, Karl and Maria had their first son at Mount Sinai Hospital in Toronto. The couple didn't have a name picked out for their new baby boy. During her stay in the hospital, Maria saw a magazine article about one of her favourite characters on the hit TV show *Bonanza*. The actor who played Adam Cartwright was named Pernell Roberts. Maria and Karl liked the sound of the name. So the first Subban son was given the first name Pernell. It was a Hollywood star's name for a little boy who would become a celebrity himself one day. The baby's full name was Pernell Karl Sylvester Subban. Karl for his father and Sylvester was to honour his grandfather. The family started using the nickname P.K. almost right away.

2 Reaching for the Stars

A growing family, the Subbans bought a home in Toronto's Rexdale neighbourhood. Karl had fulfilled his dream of becoming a teacher and Maria worked as an office administrator. Karl worked a lot of hours to support his young family. He had two teaching jobs. He taught during the day at an elementary school and was also the vice-principal of a night school program at Runnymede Collegiate.

P.K.'s older sisters loved having a baby brother to fuss over. Natasha helped him learn to skate. In fact, the first pair of skates P.K. put on at two-and-a-half years old were a pair of Natasha's figure skates. His first few attempts on the ice were pretty shaky, but before long P.K. was taking off over the frozen surface. It seemed like he was born to be on skates!

Karl and Maria both believed that their time and attention was the most important thing they could give their kids. And Karl felt that different sports were something his kids could feel confident about. But when it came time to relax in front of the TV, they watched hockey. Little P.K. would get very excited and run around the living room whenever a hockey game came on the TV. From the early days when he was very young, P.K. told his parents he wanted to play hockey, just like the guys on TV.

Nathan Phillips Square, Toronto, Ontario.

Once P.K. started skating, Karl wanted to get him out on the ice as much as possible. He came up with a plan to help P.K. learn how to skate that wouldn't cost any money. P.K. was going to kindergarten in the afternoon while Karl worked all day at school and into the evening, teaching night school. After Karl returned home, he would wake up P.K., who had gone to bed in his snowsuit so he would be ready to go. Karl would drive them into the city centre to Nathan Phillips Square in front of Toronto's city hall. The square had an outdoor rink that was the first to open in the late fall for public skating. Once the adults left for the night, P.K. and Karl would take over the ice. They would skate from 10 pm to 1 or 2 am under the lights of the three arches over the rink. For P.K. it was like skating right under the stars. As a treat, P.K. and Karl always got a slice of pizza afterward. Karl would bring P.K. home and carry his sleeping son into the house. Maria would put P.K. to bed and then wake him up in the late morning, just in time to catch the bus to school.

The thing P.K. liked most in the world was to skate. The boy would skate all day long if he could. Karl and Maria knew that for their children to succeed, practice was necessary. So when the Subbans moved to a house with a big yard, Karl turned their backyard into a skating rink. All winter long, P.K. spent as much time as he could in his backyard paradise.

Famous Outdoor Skating Rinks Around the World

Grab your skates and visit some of these incredible ice-skating rinks:

- The Rink at Rockefeller Center, New York City, US
- GUM Skating Rink, Moscow, Russia
- Tower of London Ice Rink, London, England
- Rideau Canal Skateway, Ottawa, Canada
- McCormick Tribune Ice Rink, Chicago, US
- Ice Park Skating Rink, Helsinki, Finland

The Subban household was a busy one, since there was a new baby. P.K.'s brother Malcolm was born on December 21, 1993. That year P.K. was only four years old, but he began playing house-league hockey. P.K. was signed up to play with the Flames in the Chris Tonks arena. The night before P.K.'s first game, Karl brought home a bag of hockey gear that some teachers at his school had donated. P.K. was so excited he couldn't sit still. Karl was a little worried as he pulled pieces of hockey equipment from the bag. He had no idea what most of it was for!

The first few weeks P.K. played hockey, both Karl and P.K. were learning more about the game. Still struggling with the gear, Karl decided to get P.K. into his gear at home and to drive him to the games already dressed. P.K. was playing with kids a couple of years older. He was a good skater, but still too young to understand all the aspects of playing the game. But P.K. knew one thing: he knew how to get his stick on the puck and to carry it down the ice.

3 On the Blue Line

By the time he was five years old, P.K. Subban was taking charge on the ice. He was playing on the all-star team for six-year-olds. That year the team had a 21-goal season and P.K. scored 19 of those 21 goals. He was big for his age, with a strong build. Most kids his age were still learning how to balance on their skates and swinging madly at the puck. P.K. was shooting the puck hard and directing it where he wanted it to go. Other parents, shocked at P.K.'s skill level, and fans from opposing teams would ask to see his birth certificate. They couldn't believe he was only five years old. Karl said that he looked bigger too because they always

Growing up, P.K. was inspired by Canadian NHL player Bobby Orr (right), who played defence for the Boston Bruins in 1966–79.

bought P.K.'s equipment a size too big so that he could grow into it!

When P.K. was six, Karl decided to sign him up for a select team with the Etobicoke Hockey League. He was added to the all-star lineup, playing with the Super 8s. At the age of six, P.K. was firing such powerful shots that he once cracked the helmet of a goalie. The goalie left the game and decided being a netminder was not for him. Karl found out later that the Super 8 team was for eight-year-olds. P.K. was too young, but he was more than able to compete with kids two years older than he was.

Wrong Way Subban

Karl recalls a brief time when P.K. was just starting to play, he would skate the wrong direction with the puck — into his own zone! For that, P.K. got the nickname Wrong Way. But it didn't last for very long.

It was during this time that P.K. discovered the NHL player who would inspire him in many ways. Bobby Orr was an NHL superstar who played most of his career with the Boston Bruins. Bobby played from 1966–1979 when he was forced to retire due to injuries. "Number Four, Bobby Orr" became P.K.'s favourite player. A fellow Canadian, Orr invented a style of playing defence that changed the game of hockey forever. He was a two-way player. He could defend his goaltender, but he could also skate to the opposite end and score. Many hockey fans today still believe he is the greatest hockey player of all time.

P.K. loved to watch video tapes of him playing. Like Orr, P.K. had the skill and the size needed to defend the net. He could also rush up the ice with the puck and score. Even as a kid he was perfecting his slapshot! A friend of Karl's once told

P.K.'s Etobicoke Hockey Team Photo.

him that teams were always looking for good defencemen. It was becoming clear that P.K. was perfect for the position.

It was during his early years at the rink that P.K. first learned about **racism**. P.K. remembers being just eight years old, crying as he came out of the dressing room at the Vaughan Iceplex. He told his dad that a boy on the ice called him the N-word. Karl told him there was no need to cry because it was only a word. He reminded P.K. of the old rhyme: "Sticks and stones can break

On Defence

Defencemen can also be called, "D," "D-men" or blueliners. Here are some of the best defencemen in the NHL.

Past: Red Kelly, Tim Horton, Bobby Orr, Borje Salming, Al MacInnis, Rob Blake, Scott Niedermayer, Ray Bourque

Present: Drew Doughty, Victor Hedman, Erik Karlsson, Brent Burns, Roman Josi, Dustin Byfuglien, Kris Letang, Seth Jones

my bones but names can never hurt me." Even so, P.K. became very aware of the pain that hateful name-calling can cause.

As P.K.'s love of hockey grew, so did the Subban family. On March 3, 1995, Jordan was born. P.K. was a big brother for the second time. Now the Subban family was complete with P.K. right in the middle. Just as P.K. was inspired by Bobby Orr, he would go on to inspire his little brothers to play the same game he adored.

Before long, hockey was an almost daily event in the Subban household. Karl and Maria, along with all their children, seemed to be in hockey arenas all the time. P.K.'s eldest sister, Nastassia, remembers that when she was buying her first car, she tested out the trunk first to make sure her brother's hockey gear would fit in it!

P.K. was becoming a force to be noticed on the ice, but his dad insisted that school had to come first. Karl was known for being a strict teacher, and he made sure his children kept up with their work at school. Later in his career Karl would become a school principal at some of the toughest schools in Toronto's west end. He was known for running his schools with a strict passion. P.K. would later tell hockey writer and broadcaster Paul Romanuk that, as a kid, "If I didn't do well in school, I didn't get to play hockey."

4 Minor-League Challenges

As P.K. grew older and played for different teams, the Subban family found themselves in many different arenas in the Greater Toronto Hockey League (**GTHL**). Karl and Maria would often realize they were the only black family in the arena. One rink that P.K. remembers as a special place to play is the Herbert H. Carnegie Arena on Finch Avenue West in Toronto. The arena was named in honour of legendary black Canadian hockey player Herbert

Carnegie, who played during the 1940s and 1950s. Carnegie was never allowed to play in the NHL because of the colour of his skin.

Painting of Herbert Carnegie in his Quebec Aces uniform as seen in the Herbert Carnegie Arena in Toronto, Ontario.

When P.K. was 10 years old and playing for the elite AAA Toronto Red Wings, a situation with a coach was out of control. Karl and Maria watched from the stands night after night as their son was yelled at, left out of drills and benched during games. Finally, Karl had enough and yelled to P.K. to get off the ice. It was the first time Karl had interfered in a game. Officials, parents and other spectators were all stunned. P.K. went to the dressing room to change, and the Subbans left the arena.

Karl and Maria knew that this form of bullying was affecting P.K. They had to do something about it. Karl said later that he was wrong to take P.K. out of a game situation, but he couldn't just stand by and watch his son be picked on. He wanted hockey to be fun for P.K.

Represent!

Canadian Grant Fuhr was the first black goaltender in the NHL. Grant was also the first black hockey player to have his name on the Stanley Cup, and to be inducted into the Hockey Hall of Fame (HHOF). Grant won five Stanley Cups while in net for the Edmonton Oilers. Canadian Angela James, who was born in 1964, was known as the Wayne Gretzky of women's hockey. In 2010 she was one of the first two women and the second black athlete to be inducted into the Hockey Hall of Fame.

The Subbans did not want P.K. to return to the Toronto Red Wings. They made a deal to swap with another player who wanted a change of teams. P.K. went to the Mississauga Reps and a player from the Reps went to the Red Wings. People began spreading nasty rumours about the Subbans, saying that they had "played the race card" to get P.K. on his new team. Many people were angry about the trade and blamed P.K.'s troubles on the fact that he was black.

P.K. was just happy to be back playing hockey again. But the family knew he'd have to face his old team on the ice eventually. Word was out that the Red Wings were going to "take out" P.K. when they got the chance at the next game.

That chance never came. When he faced his old team, P.K. was ready for the

Old Friends Become Opponents

When P.K. turned pro, he found himself face-to-face with many players he'd played with in the Greater Toronto Hockey League. At the age of nine, he played on the North York Junior Canadiens with teammate Steven Stamkos. Another friend from the GTHL was John Tavares, who was also on Team Canada's World Junior squad with P.K. when the boys were teenagers.

challenge. He played one of his best games in his minor hockey career against the Red Wings. It was like a fairy tale coming true. He scored four goals and got an assist on the fifth goal as the Reps upset the Red Wings in a 5–1 win!

According to the canadianencyclopedia.ca P.K. faced ongoing racism throughout this time. P.K. was once told by a coach that he would never be successful in hockey. Upon hearing this, Karl Subban told his son, "There are three senses you need to understand to make it into hockey: hockey sense, common sense and nonsense. You use your hockey sense on the ice, you use your common sense off the ice, and you have to know what to do with the nonsense, because a lot of it is nonsense."

Keeping P.K. in Sticks

Karl Subban told newspaper reporter Sean Fitz-Gerald that P.K. broke a lot of sticks in his minor hockey days. P.K. said in the same interview that he tried to break sticks on purpose so that he could get a new one! "I was one of those kids. And now I realize: 'Wow, I can't believe my parents had to shell out that type of money,'" P.K. admitted in the interview.

5 School Days and Hockey Dreams

The Subban household was always busy, with Karl and Maria sharing the duties of raising their young family. P.K.'s schedule was one of the most challenging and he had to keep on top of all his commitments. P.K. worked as hard at being a good student as he did on his hockey skills.

P.K.'s childhood friend Sophie Giorno remembers him as a happy kid. The two friends first met at Humbercrest Junior Public School and remained friends all the way through high school. "P.K. always had a bright smile on his face," Sophie recalls. "When he walked down the hallway at school he'd say 'hi' to everyone. He never seemed down."

"A whole group of us used to walk home together after school," Sophie has said. "We had lots of fun laughing and joking together." One of their favourite things to do together was to take a short–

Runnymede C.I. Sports Stars

P.K.'s high school produced a number of top athletes including:

- Jim Peplinski, captain of the Calgary Flames during their 1988–89 Stanley Cup-winning season

- Dick Aldridge, linebacker for the Toronto Argonauts and the Hamilton Tiger-Cats

- Darren Thomas, member of the 1988 Olympic basketball team

cut on their way home from school. During the winter months they came up with a faster way to cut through the valley to their west-end neighbourhood. "The hill was really steep and it would be covered in snow and slippery to walk on. So we all decided to slide down the hill on our bottoms — it was really fun!"

P.K. began high school at Runnymede Collegiate Institute in Toronto. The staff remembered him as a polite, good-natured student. One teacher who spent a lot of time with P.K. was his Physical Education teacher, Mr. Rowland. In addition to teaching classes, Coach Rowland also coached the high school hockey team. P.K. played on the Ravens hockey team in his grade 9 year.

The coach has said that P.K. had highly developed hockey skills and was a great all-around athlete. "He could play any sport at a high level," said Coach Rowland. He recalled P.K. playing AAA hockey at the same time for the North York Rangers. "His father, Karl, would make sure that P.K. could make practices with the school team on Mondays and Thursdays after school, and then rush him to wherever his other team was playing or practicing." What most impressed Coach Rowland was how hard P.K. worked to improve his skills. "P.K. would skate harder, work harder on his edge and passing drills, and play more games than any other of his teammates. What I found to be his two greatest skills were his backward skating ability and his booming shot. Even back in grade 9 he had incredible hockey sense and was never afraid to rush the puck!"

School hockey teammate Christopher Tranter joins the coach as an admirer of P.K.'s hockey skill. "When P.K. joined the school hockey team in grade 9, he was one of the younger guys. Most of the players, like myself, were in grade 11 or 12 so we

P.K.'s player photo during this time with the Markham Islanders.

were a few years older than him." Christopher laughs when he says, "P.K. was a way better hockey player than any of us!" Christopher recalls that P.K. had to quit the Ravens team after the first year, to focus on

his **AAA** career. But he still remained buddies with the guys on the team.

One story from P.K.'s high school days
shows how P.K. was serious about his
future, even back then. P.K.'s grade 9
Careers teacher laughs when she reflects
on the class she taught that year. She asked
each student to do a presentation on their
future goals and aspirations. All but one
of the boys said they were going to the
NBA. One student, however, said he had
no interest in the NBA. P.K. had his sights
set on the NHL. The teacher remembers
pointing out, as gently as she could, how

P.K. and B-ball

During interviews, P.K. often talks about his
love of basketball. He says, "I could dunk
. . . I was really good!" P.K.'s father, Karl,
and his sister Nastassia were both university
basketball stars.

Runnymede
C.I. school
logo.

slight the chances were of playing in a pro sports league and having a full-time career as an athlete. She advised her students to have a backup plan. According to the teacher, P.K. didn't hesitate. He said he would work as a hockey commentator or hockey broadcaster if playing pro didn't work out for him!

6 A Home Away from Home

There is an old African **proverb** that says, "It takes a village to raise a child." This proved true for P.K. and his family as his hockey career moved forward. Karl commented that, "It also takes a village to raise an NHLer . . . to grow their potential." In an interview for the colorofhockey.com website, Karl said, "Maria and I can't stand there and say, 'Look at us, we did it all by ourselves.'" So the Subbans embraced the village around them as P.K. continued to reach for the stars.

In May 2005, just a few days before he turned 16, P.K. was **drafted** by the Belleville Bulls of the Ontario Hockey League (OHL). It was a great honour to be selected for the team, and it meant that P.K. was moving up in the hockey world. But it was also a sad time for the family. Karl would later tell *The New Yorker* reporter Ben McGrath that P.K.'s sisters cried when they heard the news. The adjustment was going to change the close-knit family in a big way because P.K. had to leave home to be closer to his new team.

Although P.K. was very excited about the opportunity to play for the Bulls, he was also a little hurt. He had been selected in the sixth round and was the 105th overall selection in the OHL draft. While some may have expected P.K. to be drafted a few rounds earlier, other players had caught up to P.K. in size, so there were opinions that P.K. was too small to be a defenceman. Some people said that he was too loud and outspoken to be a team player. The sixth round draft position meant that P.K. was not guaranteed a spot on the team. He had to train all summer to get in shape for the team camp where final cuts would be made.

P.K. was up for the challenge. He was determined to show who he really was and what he was capable of. P.K. made it through the camp and signed with the team. For his Belleville Bulls jersey he took the number six to remind himself that he had to do everything he could to be seen as more than a sixth-round draft. He had to work harder and keep reaching for those stars.

The city of Belleville is located on the north shore of the Bay of Quinte. It was about 180 km (115 miles) from P.K.'s family home in Toronto. His new life in Belleville would continue to revolve around school

P.K. breaks his stick during a Belleville Bulls vs. London Knights game January 31, 2009.

and hockey. P.K. enrolled in high school and as a young and enthusiastic student athlete, balanced things well between his workload and his athletic training both on and off the ice.

Leaving his family behind in Toronto was tough for P.K. Luckily he was one of the players who found a home away from home. P.K. was set up to live with a local family in the Belleville area. P.K. **billeted** with a Belleville city employee named Amy McMillan and her son Johnathan. Amy became like a second mother to P.K. Maria would later say knowing Amy was there helped her to finally relax and be able to sleep at night, knowing P.K. was in good hands. Amy took her role very seriously, helping P.K. with his homework and cooking the young hockey player his meals. She even learned to make some of the Subban family recipes. Amy also took on the role of looking out for P.K. According to an article in *Toronto Life* magazine, a reporter called Amy and asked if she was ever afraid to have a young black guy living in her house. Amy immediately hung up the phone to end the call.

P.K.'s first OHL season with the Bulls got off to a slow start, but his stats showed him growing into one of the team's top blueliners. He earned 12 points in the 52 games he played in his 2005 **rookie** season with the Bulls. Over 2006–07, P.K. collected 56 points in the 68 games he played.

P.K. evades a defender from the Mississauga St.
Michael's Majors during an OHL game,
November 2, 2008.

In the 2007–08 season, P.K. played a major
role in helping the Bulls reach the Memorial
Cup playoffs, where he recorded 23 points
in 21 games. In the fourth year of his junior
career, P.K. was assistant captain for the Bulls
and achieved an incredible 76 points overall,
racking up 14 goals and 62 assists in the 56
regular games. Belleville advanced to the
playoffs that year, but lost in the semifinals to

Meeting a Hero

Gord Simmonds, former owner of the Belleville Bulls, reflects on when he was able to introduce P.K. to his hockey hero. "In 2006, the OHL All-Star Game was in Belleville and Bobby Orr was there to make the ceremonial puck drop. P.K. had asked me to introduce him," recalls Gord. "I did the introduction and the two of them sat side by side watching the game together."

the Brampton Battalion. P.K. left his mark in Belleville as the top point-producing defenceman in Belleville Bulls history!

In an ontariohockeyleague.com 2019 interview, former Belleville Bulls coach and General Manager George Burnett recalls, "P.K. has always had a big personality. He met every challenge with tremendous commitment and work and you never questioned how hard he competed." Burnett talks about P.K.'s offensive skills, but says, "He also took a lot of pride in playing the game the right way defensively too and I think that aspect of his game only got better as his time in Belleville progressed."

In the same interview, Karl and Maria spoke about how lucky P.K. was to be surrounded by a great group of people who helped him along the way. Karl said that his son had great support and guidance from people like George Burnett and his staff, the McMillan family and the entire Belleville community.

Although P.K. and his family received love and support from the Belleville community, there were still instances of racism. George Burnett mentions that there were times P.K. could have exploded over comments being made. But P.K. always chose to take the high road, be the bigger man and not let the taunts get to him. "I think it was a reflection of what his mom and dad had taught him," says Burnett.

7 From a Bull to a Bulldog and Beyond

P.K.'s high energy and dedication to his game finally paid off in June 2007, when he was invited to the NHL draft in Columbus, Ohio. The Belleville Bulls blueliner was selected in the second round, 43rd overall. He was picked to play in the NHL! P.K. was drafted by the Montreal Canadiens, a legendary hockey team and his Dad's all-time favourite.

The Draft

In the NHL, the top 10 draft picks have an 85 per cent chance of having a successful pro career. Top 30 picks have a 65 per cent chance. Picks outside of the top 90 have only a 15 per cent chance.

P.K. remembered holding back tears when he heard his name over the speakers in the arena. He hugged his parents and siblings and walked with the self-confidence that had grown in his time with the Bulls. Stu Cowan of the *Montreal Gazette* reported that as he shook hands with the Canadiens' coaching staff and their owners, P.K. said, "You guys made the right choice." P.K. has said it was the happiest night of his life.

Many people were surprised that P.K. was selected so high in the draft, but not P.K. He knew he was on his way. But he still had to work hard. P.K. would stay on with the

P.K. playing defence for the Hamilton Bulldogs.

Belleville Bulls to continue to improve his game through the 2008–09 season.

After his final season with the Bulls, P.K.'s next move was to the Hamilton Bulldogs of the American Hockey League (AHL). The Bulldogs were the Montreal Canadiens farm team, where younger players are sent to prepare to play in the NHL. P.K. continued to shine as he improved his defensive skills and his ability to score. P.K. was third in the AHL among defencemen, with a 53-point regular season that year. He would add another 10 points to that number in the AHL playoffs. One very important goal P.K. made was the one against the Manitoba Moose that gave the Bulls a 5–4 playoff win! That season P.K. made the AHL All-Star Team that played in Portland, Oregon.

During P.K.'s 2009–10 season with the Hamilton Bulldogs, he worked closely with Dan Bushey, the assistant equipment

*P.K. comes around the net during a Hamilton
Bulldogs game.*

manager for the team. Bushey remembered how hard P.K. worked on and
off the ice to prepare for their 72-game
season. He thought P.K. was the kind of
guy who made friends with everyone, "a
joker, but he could take a joke too."

Bushey chuckled as he recalled the dressing room etiquette that P.K., like all new
rookies on a team, had to learn. "There's a
pecking order in the dressing room and it's
all about respect," he explained. The older

players, the **veterans** who have played a few games in the NHL, are in charge. They have their pick of the best spots in the room. When a rookie like P.K. comes in, he would be seated between two veterans. P.K. was seated between team captain Alex Henry and Michael Glumac, "who took him under their wing and taught him all they knew about playing in the pros," said Bushey.

Even when it came to the music played in the dressing room, the older players ruled. Bushey remembered that when P.K. tried to put his rap music on, the veterans would toss his MP3 player across the room. When they really wanted to tease him they called him, "Pernell Karl." P.K. hated that! "He wanted to be called P.K.," said Bushey. But even joking in the dressing room was done with respect, he said — everyone was treated the same.

P.K. was known for coming to Dan Bushey five minutes before the **warm-up**

Praise from Someone Who Knows

Derek Wills, Calgary Flames Radio play-by-play announcer on Sportsnet 960 *The Fan*, remembers P.K. very well from his days as a Hamilton Bulldog. "P.K. was no doubt the most exciting player I saw during my 13 seasons calling American Hockey League games with the Hamilton Bulldogs. P.K. should be proud of all that he has accomplished both on and off the ice."

and often just before the team went on the ice to ask him to tape a couple of sticks for him. Bushey was never able to say no to P.K. "He's a special guy, and he has a heart of gold, so it was impossible to be mad at him."

P.K. wasn't just popular with the Bulldogs and their staff. The fans loved him too! Dan Bushey said that P.K. was one of the most popular guest speakers the team had. And P.K. would never say no to an invitation. "P.K. was always the first guy to volunteer when it came to school talks or public events," he recalled. "He was always very generous with his time."

The team that had drafted P.K. could see his hard work with the Bulls and Bulldogs. On May 5, 2009, P.K. signed a $2.625 million, three-year entry-level contract with the Montreal Canadiens. He was thrilled to be playing with the Habs. It was the team that had been his father's first introduction to hockey from the time his family arrived in Canada.

The most important achievements of P.K.'s 2009–10 season were still to come. P.K. got his first call-up to the Canadiens on February 11, 2010, and in his debut the next day he scored his first NHL point, an assist against the Philadelphia Flyers. On April 26, 2010, P.K. was recalled from Hamilton to the Canadiens for the first-round Stanley Cup Playoff series against the Washington Capitals. P.K. recorded his first NHL playoff point for an assist in his first NHL playoff game!

P.K.'s first goal as an NHLer came in Game 1 of the Canadiens' second-round playoff series on April 30th, 2010. In Game 3 of the Eastern Conference finals against the Philadelphia Flyers, P.K. became the third rookie defenceman in Canadiens history to record three assists in one game!

In his debut playoff run with the Canadiens, P.K. recorded one goal and eight points in 14 playoff games for the Canadiens before the Montreal Canadiens were eliminated by the Flyers. Although the NHL season was over for the Canadiens, P.K. still had a chance to keep his playoff run alive. After the Montreal season ended, P.K. returned to the Hamilton Bulldogs, who were still in their **division** playoffs for the Calder Cup. At the end of the American Hockey League season, P.K. was given the President's Award for an outstanding year in hockey with the Bulldogs!

8 Pride and Joy

It was a major source of pride for all the Subban family members when P.K. was signed to his first NHL contract. One of the first things P.K. did was buy a black Ford Expedition for his dad. P.K. told reporter Matthew Hague in a 2013 interview, "I was embarrassed to be seen in my dad's beat-up 1983 Toyota Corolla." But what P.K. was really doing with the truck was saying thank you to Karl for all he had done for him. P.K. would also thank his parents by helping them build their dream home in Nobleton, Ontario. It has its own gym and a backyard large enough for an ice rink in the wintertime!

Shortly after being drafted, P.K. took the jersey number he's most recognized for: number 76. In an interview with Stu Cowan of the *Montreal Gazette*, P.K. explained how he chose his number. "I was drafted in the sixth round in junior, which is why I originally wore the number 6, so I kept part of that in my number here. The number 7 was because I was drafted in 2007."

P.K. proudly wore his number 76 jersey for Montreal. And he wore the Maple Leaf proudly for his country a number of times too. He first played on Team Canada at the 2008 International Ice Hockey Federation (IIHF) World Junior Championship in Pardubice, Czech Republic, where Canada won the gold medal.

P.K. during the Team Canada vs Russia World Junior Championships in Ottawa, Canada, 2009.

P.K.'s former Belleville Bulls coach George Burnett remembered the joy and pride P.K. felt when he called to tell him he had made the Team Canada roster. Burnett felt it had a truly Canadian moment. "I was sitting in a Tim Hortons drive-through when P.K. called to tell me he had made the Canadian World Junior team for the first time. He had been a long shot to make the team, as he was only 18 years old. P.K. was thrilled to have his first opportunity to **represent** Canada in this most prestigious event during the holiday season. I reminded him of the special honour it was to represent Canada in any event and that any role big or small was very important. I told him, even if he didn't play much — or if he was asked to just provide support on the bench or carry the pucks, for that matter — to do it to the best of his ability without hesitation. P.K. played a limited role. But along with Bulls teammate Shawn Matthias, who played a very significant role on the team, they were so proud to return to Belleville with their medals."

P.K. returned for the 2009 World Junior Championship in Ottawa as an assistant captain for Team Canada. Burnett said, "P.K. played a significant role this time around and again helped Canada win gold. This was certainly one of the most memorable Canadian wins in tournament history. As a coach you only hope to play a small part in helping players. The players are the ones who make the many sacrifices necessary, who make the commitment and ultimately do the work to succeed. These are always special calls and memories to cherish as a coach." P.K. helped his team win a second straight gold medal and he was named to the media tournament all-star team, thanks to his three goals and six assists.

The non-believers had been silenced. P.K.'s outstanding play had removed all doubt that he was the real thing. He might have been picked way down in the draft,

P.K. and John Tavares show off their 2009 World Junior Championship rings.

but P.K. had broken through. He was a difference maker and he wasn't going to let anything stop him!

But not everyone was a P.K. fan. A number of sportswriters and fans criticized him on TV and social media. Some reporters thought that P.K. was attacked so often in the media because he was a black hockey player, competing in the very white game of NHL hockey. Even through his personal career gains, P.K. was still facing the ugly world of racism. It was a subject that P.K. usually chose not to comment on.

Being the Change

P.K. has not been inducted into the Hockey Hall of Fame, but he is part of HHOF's Hometown Hockey Zone in an exhibit called The Changing Face of Hockey — Diversity in Our Game. Izak Westgate, manager of outreach exhibits and assistant curator at the Hockey Hall of Fame, talks about P.K.'s popularity with fans. "P.K. is one of the more popular athletes in the game today with everything he does for the game, as well as his energetic and enthusiastic personality. So any time we take his **artifacts** on the road, kids in particular always gravitate to them due to the recognition factor," explains Izak.

9 Je T'aime, Montreal!

P.K. fell in love with Montreal. Playing for the red, white and blue just felt right. After all, it was his dad's favourite team. To some it seemed to be a bit of an odd fit. P.K. was from the rival city of Toronto, he didn't speak French and he was a player of colour. But Canadiens fans learned very quickly that the 6-foot, 210-pound offensive-defenceman was there to win!

P.K. fit in perfectly with the Montreal lifestyle. Food, fashion and fun were part of the city's culture and P.K. was into the vibe the city had going on. He loved the food and became good friends with one of Montreal's top chefs, Antonio Park, who owned P.K.'s favourite sushi restaurant. Smartly dressed Montrealers were everywhere and the nightlife suited P.K. just fine. He was enjoying his new home in Montreal, but he still called his parents every day and texted with his four siblings as often as possible.

The 2010–11 season was P.K.'s first full season in the NHL. He racked up 38 points, getting 14 goals and 24 assists. P.K. also led all other Canadiens players that season with nine **power-play** goals.

By the next season, P.K. had become a force on the ice for his team. In 2011–12, P.K. was the heart of the Montreal Canadiens power play (PP), leading the team in number of minutes of PP ice time at 283:04. His total ice time added up to

1,968:28 minutes and his average time on the ice per game was 24:18 minutes.

But P.K.'s brilliance on the ice was not all that hockey insiders were talking about. In January 2011, he scored a game-winning overtime goal against the Calgary Flames. P.K. was so excited that he slid down the ice in his "archer" pose to celebrate the goal. Some of P.K.'s opponents, other NHLers and people in the media did not like such a flashy display after scoring his goal.

P.K. thrilled Habs fans once again on March 20, 2011, when he made Canadiens hockey history. P.K. became the Canadiens first rookie defenceman to score three goals

Rap Track

P.K. was so popular in Montreal that local rapper Wasiu recorded a song about him and how important he was to the local black community.

A 1934–1935 hockey program from the Montreal Forum. Montreal was one of the Original Six teams that first made up the NHL.

in a game! P.K.'s **hat trick** led the Habs to a victory over the Minnesota Wild.

In his 2011–12 season, P.K. scored 38 points in the 81 games the Canadiens played. But the 2012–13 season was cut short by a player **lockout**. The lockout was due to a dispute between the NHL and the National Hockey League Players Association (NHLPA). At 11:59 p.m. on September 15, 2012, NHL hockey completely shut down in North America. The two opposing sides settled their differences four months later and hockey began again on January 6, 2013. The shortened season consisted of only 42 games. P.K. recorded 38 points in the short length of time the NHL had to play. For P.K. it meant that he had almost a point in every game he played! That season he was selected for the NHL's all-star team.

Before the lockout, P.K. had been due to sign a new contract with the Canadiens.

By the time the lockout ended, P.K. still didn't have a signed deal with the Habs. P.K. had to sit out the first four games of the season once the league started up again because he wasn't a signed player. Rumours began to spread that P.K. wanted too much money and was being greedy. Even some of his teammates were getting angry over his contract troubles. When P.K. did finally sign a two-year contract for $5.7 million, many people were still upset over the long negotiations.

But P.K. knew his worth. In his time with the Canadiens he helped them go from last place to the top of their division and then all the way to the Eastern Conference final. And he did it twice — once in 2010 against the Philadelphia Flyers and again when they faced the New York Rangers in 2014.

Game On!

On June 7, 2015, kids playing road hockey in Montreal's Westmount neighbourhood got a big surprise when P.K. and a friend got out of their car to join their game!

P.K.'s ties to the city of Montreal went beyond hockey. On September 1, 2015, P.K. made a $10 million donation to the Montreal Children's Hospital. It was the largest donation by any Canadian athlete in history. The hospital showed their appreciation for P.K.'s generous gift by naming their new hospital atrium after him. He would often stop by the hospital and surprise patients and staff with a visit. P.K. said in an interview with sportsnet.ca that seeing the *Atrium P.K. Subban* lettering as he walked in the hospital gave him goosebumps. He also committed to be spokesman for the hospital for the next seven years and to continue to raise money for them.

Despite some of the hardships he had to face on the team, P.K. loved the city of Montreal, and the city loved him right back!

10 Silencing the Haters

Over his life, P.K. learned to deal with the unfair treatment he sometimes received. Building on lessons he was taught at home, he learned to cope with racism. He taught himself how to see beyond it. P.K. did not dwell on the hatred, and he chose to rise above it. Personal attacks couldn't keep P.K. down. He didn't let the hate stop him from reaching his goals. He knew what he wanted, and his dad's words of support and encouragement kept him fighting for what he believed in and the game he loved to play.

In 2013, *Sports Illustrated* journalist Allan Muir wrote an article about the most hated players in the NHL. The top 10 list had P.K. Subban as number one. Even though P.K. was at the top of his list, Muir admitted, "The game needs more characters like him." Muir added, "It's obvious that he has bridges to rebuild, and not just because of his lengthy contract dispute . . . Subban's flashy personality on and off the ice is a break from hockey tradition, and that clearly rankles some people. Too bad."

In a May 2013 article, *Montreal Gazette* sportswriter Jack Todd asked this question: "Would P.K. be so disliked if he were white and from a small town, instead of black and from a big city?" In the same article he wrote, "Black superstars are as rare as — well, as rare as Subban. Because he's unique, Subban faces a special set of problems. The hockey world is still getting used to the idea of the black superstar — and that's where Subban has hit rough waters at times."

P.K.'s father guided him through the ugliness of the racism around him. Karl told him, "Don't let them win." Karl admitted it's easy to give that advice, but that overcoming racism takes practice, "and P.K. has had a lot of practice." P.K. doesn't like to talk about the racism he has had to face over the years. It may be that he thinks that letting the haters make him talk about it is letting them win.

P.K. was a big part of the Canadiens' success for the 2012–13 season. In an end-of-season game against the New York Islanders, P.K. blasted one of his famous slapshots at the net and scored in the second period. In the third period he put another puck behind the goalie. Montreal beat the Islanders 5–2 and finished the season at the top of their division.

P.K. proudly wore the A, for alternate captain, on his Montreal jersey during home games. As an alternate captain, it was his responsibility to speak to the referees on behalf of the team when the captain was not on the ice. As one of four players on the team to share those duties, P.K. was trusted with an important leadership role on the ice.

In June 2013, after an incredible season of 11 goals and 27 assists in 42 games, P.K. won the Norris Trophy as the NHL's top defenceman. He became the first Montreal defenceman to win the award since Chris Chelios in 1989. More importantly, he became the first black hockey player to be awarded the trophy.

On January 7, 2014, P.K. was named to play for the Canadian men's Olympic hockey team. He was thrilled to represent his country again. The Olympic Winter Games were held in Sochi, Russia, and P.K. would be playing alongside his good friend and fellow Montreal Canadien, goaltender Carey Price.

But P.K. did not get much ice time in Sochi. Coach Mike Babcock chose to go with more experienced defencemen on the **blue line**. P.K. appeared in one game at the Olympics, playing only eight minutes overall. Team Canada won the gold medal that year and P.K. was happy to have even played a small role in the series. In a 2014 interview with Ben McGrath

The Norris Trophy

The James Norris Trophy is awarded every year to the top defenceman in the league. It was named after Detroit Red Wings owner James E. Norris and was first awarded in 1954. Bobby Orr won it more times than anyone in NHL history — eight years in a row!

of *The New Yorker* magazine, P.K. said, "The Olympics is about representing your country, and if you get an opportunity to play you give it all you have. At the end of the day, we won. I got a gold medal. I don't care how I got it."

In 2014, P.K. was asked by a reporter from the *National Post* what he did with his gold medal from the Sochi Olympic Games. "My parents have it stashed away somewhere. I don't see it anymore," P.K. said. "I spent a week and a half with it, and then they took it from me. So they have it and are enjoying it now."

The New Yorker magazine reported in 2014 that in the 30 teams that made up the National Hockey League, only 18 of the players were black. P.K. was one of those players. Even the haters had a hard time ignoring what a talented hockey player he was to be in that elite group. P.K. just played even harder and was named to the all-star team for the first time, leaving no doubt that he was one of the best players in the game!

That season P.K. tied for the highest-scoring defenceman with 38 points in a 48-game season. P.K. also tied for second place in the NHL for power-play assists at 19. And he tied for the Montreal playoff scoring lead at four points. P.K. was once again signing a new contract deal with the Canadiens. After his incredible play, the Montreal Canadiens had no choice but to sign P.K. to a contract that earned him $72 million over eight years. That made the blueliner from Toronto the highest-paid defenceman in the NHL!

Sadly, all P.K.'s achievements were once again overlooked in 2014 when he was attacked on social media by angry Boston Bruins fans. The comments were hateful, racist slurs that disrespected P.K. and people of colour.

Some NHL Star Players Who are Black

Jarome Iginla, Dustin Byfuglien, Wayne Simmonds, Evander Kane, Joel Ward, Kyle Okposo, Seth Jones, Emerson Etem, Devante Smith-Pelly, Chris Stewart, Trevor Daley, Johnny Oduya, Darnell Nurse, Anthony Duclair

When the Boston Bruins fans went on the attack after P.K. and the Canadiens had knocked them out of the Stanley Cup quarter-finals, P.K. responded with a brilliant comeback. On May 22, 2014, P.K. told reporter Charlie Gillis, "I don't really care what the other team thinks. I don't care what their fans think. If they hate me, great. Hate me. We'll just keep winning, I'll just keep scoring and we'll move on."

11 What You See Is What You Get!

P.K. has been called many names over his career, but he likes to call himself the Subbanator. He calls his fans the Subbanation. If there is one thing that is true about P.K. and his style it is that what you see is what you get. He's no phony. If he makes a promise or takes on a challenge he follows through.

P.K. has always had a strong personality and doesn't shy away from attention.

He is a one-man media machine. He has more than a million followers on Twitter and almost that many on his Instagram account. P.K. loves being on TV and has been on talk shows, radio broadcasts and even comedy programs. He has also appeared on NHL sportscaster panels. He's one of the most recognized faces in the NHL.

P.K. does not apologize for who he is or how he sees the game. Some hockey fans don't like when he speaks out or critiques the game. Hockey is one of the oldest organized sports in the world and can be very set in its ways. Hockey players are expected to behave in a certain way. They tend to be more reserved, less outspoken. But P.K. was never like that. When he feels things aren't right he speaks out about what needs to change. At a young age, he learned how to stand up for himself and for others too.

The "Celly"bration!

It's what you see a hockey player do after he or she has scored a goal — they celebrate! Some players' moves are unique, from jumping up on the glass, saluting the crowd or pumping their fists.

P.K. became very aware of the unfair advantages some children have over others, especially in hockey. Players from lower-income families just can't afford to play ice hockey in organized leagues. P.K. wanted to do something about it, so he got involved with Hyundai Hockey Helpers. In an interview on CBC Toronto's *Metro Morning*, P.K. explained what he was doing to help more kids play hockey. "Hyundai and KidSport have teamed up to give kids grants so that they can afford to play and pay for registration. This is our third year doing this program and we've already put 5,000 kids into the game of hockey." When P.K.

was asked why he got involved, he replied, "For these kids, they just want to have fun, and everyone should have the opportunity to play organized sports. There shouldn't be a gap there. There shouldn't be any barriers there."

Without a doubt, one of hockey's most outspoken personalities was *Hockey Night in Canada*'s Don Cherry. Don has criticized P.K. for everything from his style of play to his fashion sense. But his comments can confuse hockey fans, because you often hear him praise P.K. too. In

Hockey Grapes

Donald S. Cherry, also known as Grapes, is a Canadian hockey broadcaster and team owner, who also played hockey and coached for many years. Don hosted Coach's Corner on CBC TV's *Hockey Night in Canada* from the 1980s to 2019. He is well-known for his individual clothing style and sometimes surprising comments.

many ways P.K. and Don Cherry are very much alike. Flashy dressers with outspoken personalities!

In a 2014 interview for *The New Yorker* magazine, Don said that P.K. had to "stop that silly stuff like taunting other players or the way he celebrates a goal, the bow-and-arrow stuff." Don went on, "You irritate the other players and all that. You can't do that and expect the players to like you." But in the same interview Don said that P.K. had a booming shot that he called a "howitzer," the name of a big, powerful gun.

Over the years Don has also criticized P.K.'s technique for delivering his powerful bodychecks. Most players use their upper body when checking, but P.K. uses his butt. He turns his back, putting his body in the way to keep the other player away from the puck. P.K. explained in a 2014 interview with *Sports Illustrated*,

"Your butt and your back are two of the strongest parts of your body." That's why he uses them to make his checks count.

But calling a player on these things doesn't mean Don doesn't like him. During another interview with *The New Yorker*, Don described P.K. like this: "He's great for hockey. And if you ever talk to him personally, he's the most polite, nicest kid. You'd want him for a son, you know what I mean?"

National Post reporter Sean Fitz-Gerald asked P.K. if Don Cherry confused him. P.K. smiled and said, "Don Cherry is one of the most important people to the game of hockey. And what he's done for the game of hockey, and what he's still doing, he's put hockey on a platform. So, good or bad, whenever Don Cherry talks about P.K. Subban, I'm honoured to hear that . . . Whether he's ripping me or complimenting me, it's the biggest compliment to me as a player just to know that Don Cherry had something to say about me. Because I remember Don talking about Bobby Orr, Wayne Gretzky, Mario Lemieux — the best players to ever play the game. And when I think that he has something to say about me, it's a great feeling."

ESPN.com reporter Chuck Gormley pointed out to P.K. that people are always saying the NHL needs more colourful players. And then one comes along and they say he's too colourful. Chuck wanted to know how P.K. deals with that. P.K. gave a straight, honest answer. "A lot of things are said about me. And maybe if I didn't play in Montreal to start my career, a lot of those things would not have made news. But when you're in Montreal, everything gets kind of blown up and everything becomes news, which is fine. None of that stuff ever really bothered me

. . . [People] may not think how I play the game is the right way. Or they may not think everything I do is truly authentic and real, but that's just life. What are you going to do? All you do is continue to work on yourself every day as a player and as a person, and that's it. I try to get better every day and continue to do good things, not just for myself, but for the people around me, and just create good energy around me wherever I go. Because that's the only way to live, in my opinion."

12 A Devastating Trade

On June 29, 2016, at 3:54 p.m. the Montreal Canadiens made a shocking trade that surprised hockey fans everywhere. The trade was a straight swap. Montreal all-star defenceman P.K. Subban would go to the Nashville Predators in exchange for all-star defenceman Shea Weber coming to the Canadiens. This wasn't an ordinary trade in the hockey world — this was a blockbuster trade that no one saw coming. The Habs had traded away one of the most popular **defencemen** they had ever had.

P.K. was on vacation when the trade announcement was made. He told ESPN.com that he'd heard all the rumours about the team trading him, but he felt that he was safe in his position with the team. Just six days before the trade, Marc Bergevin, general manager of the Canadiens, had denied that he was looking to trade P.K. before his no-trade clause kicked in on July 1st, Canada Day.

A Thank-You Letter

Shortly after P.K. was traded, a fan named Dr. Charles Kowalski purchased a page in the *Montreal Gazette* newspaper to thank P.K. for all he had done for the city. "You are an amazing and influential role model for my children and I am going to miss not having you as a Montreal Canadien," wrote the doctor.

Carey Price in net, April 5, 2017 at the KeyBank Center for the Montreal vs. Buffalo Sabres game.

Some people suggested that management found P.K.'s outspokenness hard to handle. Others said that his personality was too big for the dressing room. In the days that followed, Bergevin refused to talk about the team's decision and stated, "I don't want to answer anymore P.K. questions."

Many Montreal fans were shocked and angry when the trade was announced.

They were stunned that the owners and management would trade away one of their star players. P.K. had scored more than 50 points in each of the three seasons he played with Montreal and in his best season with the team, 2014–15, he had 60 points. Overall P.K. had a total of 63 goals and 215 assists in the 434 games he played with the Canadiens. Fans had even thought that P.K. should have been made captain of the team instead of Max Pacioretty. Many people believed that, together with goaltender Carey Price, Subban would return the Canadiens to their glory days as the winningest team in NHL history.

Banner from the Nashville All-Star Game, January 31, 2016.

P.K. and Carey were good friends and they believed they could win it together too. Carey was one of the first people P.K. spoke to after the trade announcement was made. It was an emotional goodbye between the two friends.

In a podcast interview with the colorofhockey.com, Karl Subban said he had to change the channel on the TV when the Canadiens announced they were trading P.K. But P.K. acted in a very professional and polite manner. Shortly after the trade was announced, he told Nashville reporters, "Right now I'm going to a team that wants me." He said that he felt that he was "a whole lot closer" to winning a Stanley Cup with Nashville than he was with Montreal.

P.K. kept quiet during most of the trade comments, but he did admit one regret to reporter Brendan Kelly of the *Montreal Gazette*. "What I'm upset about and at the time [of the trade]," he said, "What I was

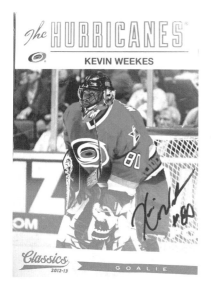

Signed player card for Kevin Weekes — goaltender for the Carolina Hurricanes.

upset about was that I had made a promise to the city when I was drafted, to bring a Stanley Cup back. And never once did I remove myself from that statement or back away from it."

Rumours were being spread that P.K.'s race played a part in the decision to trade him. In a May 2017 interview with journalist Rob Williams of the dailyhive.com, former NHL goaltender Kevin Weekes called P.K. hockey's first "fully black" superstar. Kevin knew what it felt like to be a black player in the NHL. He said he was certain race played a part in P.K. being traded. "It definitely had a role," Weekes said. "Because it's had a role ever since he came in. I know, because I've lived it. And because I live it."

At the time of the trade, Canadiens head coach Michel Therrien said that the player swap would make Montreal "a better team now." The Canadiens had a 13-1-1 start to the 2016–2017 season, but then started losing. Eight months after the trade, Michel Therrien was fired by the team.

Hidden Racism

Thehockeywriters.com posted an article in February 2018 called "Is Hockey for Everyone? Confronting Racism in the NHL." The article talked about how a fan had posted a comment on Twitter about P.K. calling him a "Monday." The Urban Dictionary website describes the term "as another way of saying the N-word without getting caught."

13 Predators Find a Star from the North

Some people thought the move to Nashville, Tennessee might be just the thing for P.K. He was now officially part of the city nicknamed Smashville, where music and entertainment are a way of life. And it suited P.K. just fine! In Montreal hockey is worshipped, and not much has changed from the Original Six traditions. But Nashville is a fairly new team in the league and hockey is just another form of entertainment.

Being brought up a Canadiens fan was a Subban family tradition, but when P.K. was traded to Nashville, the family had a new team to cheer for. And P.K. soon found that the Nashville Predators were ready to welcome him with open arms.

P.K. said in an interview with colorofhockey.com, "I didn't think there was anything better [than playing for Montreal] until I got to Nashville, and then I said 'Wow! It's so different and a great experience.' It's the music there, the environment. After the game, the honkytonks, the bars, the food. I love country music." On July 17, 2016, P.K. was spotted in a local nightclub singing Johnny Cash's "Folsom Prison Blues" and fitting right in with the Nashville music scene.

On October 1, 2016, P.K. made his pre-season debut with the team in front of a sellout crowd. P.K. had known the fans were loud in Nashville, but now the

A Funny Guy

P.K. is known for his cheerful personality and sense of humour. In 2017 when the Predators and Sidney Crosby's Pittsburgh Penguins were battling it out in a playoff finals game, the two players exchanged words. They chirped each other throughout the game. After the game, P.K. told reporters that Sidney was chirping him about having bad breath — an odd thing for players to scrap about. At the next game, P.K. arrived at the arena with a bunch of bottles of mouthwash. Anything for a joke!

cheers included him too! A couple of weeks later, on opening night of the regular season, P.K. scored his first goal with the Predators in a win against Chicago.

Unfortunately P.K. suffered an injury and didn't return to play until January 20, 2017. He missed 16 games. Even though he was injured, he was selected to represent the Predators as the captain of the Central Division in the NHL All-Star Game.

It wasn't until March 2nd that P.K. made the trip back to Montreal to play against his former team. He received an emotional tribute from Montreal fans. More than 21,000 fans cheered "P.K., P.K., P.K." as the giant scoreboard played highlights from his career with the Canadiens. Tears ran down P.K.'s face as he smiled and waved to the fans. Many of the Montreal fans were still wearing their Canadiens jerseys with the Subban name on the back.

In Montreal, many fans still weren't convinced that trading P.K. was a good move for the team. A group of dedicated P.K. followers gathered to watch his games at a local restaurant. The group was made up of 30 fans of West Indian descent living in Montreal, proud to see a player of Caribbean heritage making a difference in the big leagues.

What was special about this group of Montreal fans was that they switched to wearing P.K.'s Nashville jersey to watch his games. In June 2017, original member of the group Ryan Weekes told Cristina Ledra, a writer for NHL.com, why P.K. still has so many fans in Montreal. "He's become an icon in Montreal for a lot of the black people and young hockey players. They all look up to him for not only what he does on the ice but off the ice. And for us being black people who have watched the sport for so many years, seeing someone of his nature come into the sport and being such a great athlete, philanthropist, everything in general, it's something we're very proud of."

P.K. also continued to feel close ties with the city of Montreal. He made a special trip back to the city to announce that his P.K.'s Helping Hand fund had raised $1.4 million to support more than 9,000 families whose lives had met financial troubles due a child's illness.

During the 2018 NHL Awards, it was announced that P.K. would be on the video game cover of EA Sports *NHL 2019*. He was the first black player to be given the high-profile honour. In an interview in June 2018 with NHL.com, P.K. talked about being selected. "Growing up, and still to this day, my friends and I love seeing who is on the cover and ultimately getting to play the game. Being the cover athlete for *NHL 19*, for me, represents growth within our sport, embracing different personalities, and showing that anything is possible. I'm honoured to be able to sport the Smashville colours on this year's cover."

It wasn't a surprise to many people that P.K.'s first season with the Preds was incredible. P.K. got 10 goals and 30 assists in 66 games in the regular season. He finished the season as one of the top–10 scoring defencemen. Then he had 2 goals and 10 assists in 22 playoff games, and played a major role in helping the Predators make it all the way to the Stanley Cup finals.

P.K.'s Fashion File

P.K. doesn't just have great moves on the ice. Off the ice he's a pretty cool dude too. He's known as one of the best-dressed NHLers, with his own unique sense of fashion.

His marketing company, P.K.S.S., has landed him business partnerships with Bridgestone, Gatorade, Air Canada and RW&CO. In 2019, the *Sports Illustrated* list of the Fashionable 50 included P.K. Subban as an icon of the well-dressed athlete.

14 Strong Mind, Strong Body

P.K. has a strong belief in keeping both his mind and his body in peak condition.

From his childhood days on the ice at local arenas to the NHL, P.K. has always come prepared to play and to give it his all. For P.K., being ready to compete on the ice takes a lot of hard work and preparation long before the season starts. He spends much of the **off-season** preparing for the upcoming year.

P.K. often comes home to Toronto to

continue his personal workout system. In a 2013 interview for *Toronto Life* magazine, P.K. told reporter Matthew Hague how his off-season training works. P.K. trains with Clance Laylor at a gym in the heart of the city. Clance was a former sprinter who had to give up his athletic career because of an injury. The workout Clance prepared for the hockey star is tough, including hours of weightlifting and cardio workout routines. P.K. would have to walk across the downtown park they used for training carrying 260-pound weights or pulling a weight sled.

P.K. is very proud of his physical abilities and happily shares his workout routines on videos he posts on YouTube. Many of his followers comment that he seems to be getting stronger as he gets older. This is impressive, since you usually expect an athlete to slow down as they age.

Holy Cow

When P.K. first entered the NHL, he would often drop by his parents' house and Karl would happily barbecue a steak and some vegetables at 7:00 a.m. for his son. At the beginning of a hockey season, P.K. would order a whole butchered cow to be delivered to his parents' home. His mom, Maria, would prepare the meat for him all season. P.K. would eat the whole cow by the time the season was over!

In 2016 P.K. shared his workout routine with *New York Times* reporter John Ortved. P.K. called his routine "Barebones: chin-up bar, treadmill, free weights and mats." He described his workout gear as "an old T-shirt and compression shorts."

When Ortved asked P.K. what his goal was, he replied, "It's very important that you have enough mass to last your whole season, building my body in a way that can last, to be just as full of a player in Game 82 as I am in Game 1." When it comes to what P.K. puts in his body he told Ortved that his diet is really healthy. "I eat clean food, organic food," explained P.K. "People just need to know that I work as hard, if not harder than the guy next to me."

In a 2019 interview with *People* magazine, P.K. once again was working hard to prepare for the upcoming season. "In the off-season when I'm not skating as much, I'm able to do a lot more in the gym," P.K. told reporter Julie Mazziotta. "I lift during the season, but definitely prioritize it more in the summer. If you're in really good shape going into the season, you can maintain a lot of strength while on the ice. This way, I'm able to focus on building speed and agility." P.K. also mentioned a unique training move he does with his fiancée, World Cup skier Lindsey Vonn.

With Lindsey in a squatting position, P.K. pulls her around the rink, using an elastic that attaches to P.K.'s waist! Their dog Lucy watches from the bench.

Pre-game Meals

Athletes have to take good care of their bodies, especially what they put in them. For hockey players, pre-game meals are very important. Most players eat chicken, beef or salmon with brown rice and veggies. But others have some odd favourites:

- Sidney Crosby likes to eat peanut butter and jelly sandwiches.

- Claude Giroux prefers grilled cheese sandwiches, just like his mom used to make.

- Before a game, Wayne Gretzky used to eat four hotdogs with mustard and onions.

15 A Subban Family Hat Trick

P.K.'s first NHL hat trick was in 2011 when he was a rookie with the Montreal Canadiens. But the Subban family has scored a hat trick of their very own in the NHL. P.K. and his two younger brothers, Malcolm and Jordan, are all NHL players! Following up on big brother P.K.'s incredible NHL career, Malcolm Subban is a goaltender for the Vegas Golden Knights and Jordan, under contract with the Toronto Maple Leafs, plays with their AHL team, the Toronto Marlies.

Jordan, P.K. and Malcolm (left to right). Jordan and P.K. both play defence, Malcolm is a goaltender.

When it comes to hockey, P.K. led the way for his brothers. Ontario Hockey League photographer Aaron Bell has taken thousands of pictures of the game of hockey in his career. Some of his fondest memories are from his time with the Belleville Bulls. Aaron recalled P.K. working hard on the ice at the rink, while his little brothers, Malcolm and Jordan, ran around the arena. As they grew, both Malcolm and Jordan would sign with the team and spend their OHL careers with the Belleville Bulls, following in their big brother's footsteps — all the way to the NHL.

Karl and Maria did all they could to support the dreams of all five of the Subban children. They gave them opportunities and taught them lessons about life along the way. Money was tight for the young family, with Karl working two jobs in the early years to support his family. As the eldest boy playing hockey, P.K. was the one who got the new equipment. Malcolm and Jordan had to make do with his hand-me-downs. But that didn't matter to them — they were excited to have hockey gear.

In a 2013 interview for *Toronto Life* magazine, Karl told Matthew Hague that he let the boys practice in the living room, using the space between the piano legs as a hockey net. Karl was determined to give his kids the chance that he didn't have — to become a pro athlete. He never expected he'd score three times!

The story of this hard-working, successful family sounds like a fairy tale that came true. The Subban children are first-generation Canadians who have made their parents proud with all they achieve. The family story is so inspiring that Karl Subban wrote a book, *How We Did It: The Subban Plan for Success in Hockey, School and Life*. Karl said that he wrote the book

Subban Family Values

P.K. talks about his love of family and he's very rooted in family values. He's very close to his three nephews, Nastassia's sons, who already are on skates and love the game their uncles love to play! When the Subban family gathers together, food is always a big part of the event. Karl loves to cook for his kids and the family's favourite food is liver, cooked to Karl's secret recipe!

because people were always asking him and Maria how they did it — helped get all three of their sons into the NHL! Karl and Maria are just as proud of Nastassia and Natasha. Both Subban daughters work in education, like their dad. All five Subban children credit their parents with keeping them grounded. The Subban siblings always knew they had the full support of their parents.

In an ESPN.com interview with Chuck Gormley, P.K. explained how Karl and Maria were key to the family's success. "I'm very privileged to have great parents, caring parents, parents that dedicate a lot of their time and energy to their children, and we're very thankful for that."

Karl and Maria also taught their children important lessons on dealing with racism. Karl explained to Dan Robson, a reporter for Sportsnet, that he told his children, "You know who you are. Don't

Oh Brother!

The "Great One" Wayne Gretzky and his brother Brent played in the NHL. They are the highest-scoring brothers ever in the league, but Brent scored just one goal and four points in his short hockey career.

Here are some impressive brother combinations.

Daring Duos: Maurice (the Rocket) and Henri (Pocket Rocket) Richard, Phil and Tony Esposito, Bobby and Dennis Hull, Frank and Pete Mahovlich, Henrik and Daniel Sedin, Rich and Ron Sutter, Saku and Mikko Koivu, Brayden and Luke Schenn, Marcus and Nick Foligno, Jamie and Jordie Benn

The More the Merrier: Eric, Jordan and Marc Staal; Brian, Duane, Darryl, Brent, Rich and Ron Sutter let anything stop you." Karl said he knew that if his sons were going to make it in the NHL, they wouldn't get there because of the colour of their skin. Karl said, "They were going to make it because of their character."

16 Building Bridges and Breaking Down Barriers

P.K. Subban's personal website tells a lot about P.K. It's an inside look at the many sides of his life, on and off the ice. A quote from his site: "I have many titles but the most important one is that of a difference maker." And that is what P.K. has dedicated much of his time and money toward — making a difference.

Throughout his hockey career, P.K. has had strong beliefs about helping those less fortunate. From fundraising, to donations and devoting his personal time, P.K. has not only touched the communities where he's played hockey, but also reached out globally to help.

P.K. is known for his generous spirit. One of his first big charity projects saw him and former NHLer Georges Laraque visiting Haiti in 2011 after a devastating earthquake destroyed the country. P.K. and Georges were part of the Hockey for Haiti program that raised $1.3 million to build a temporary hospital after the main hospital was destroyed.

In 2013, helping became a family affair. Along with his father, Karl, and brothers, Malcolm and Jordan, P.K. got involved with Hyundai Hockey Helpers. The program helps support kids whose families can't afford for them to play hockey. P.K. has always been aware of how expensive it is to play hockey and knows the sacrifices his own family had to make. P.K. is also involved with the Hats Off to Kidz foundation that tries to make the lives of sick children a little happier.

When P.K. made his $10 million donation to the children's hospital in Montreal in 2015, it was through his own P.K.'s Helping Hand foundation. The foundation provides financial support for families with children who are suffering with illness. The P.K. Subban Foundation began so that P.K. could keep all his charity work organized. In Montreal, the P.K. Subban Foundation partnered with the Air Canada Foundation to build a Winter Wonderland every Christmas in the atrium of the Montreal Children's Hospital that is named for P.K.

In 2016, P.K. was given a very special award called the Meritorious Service Cross. It was presented to him by Governor General David Johnston, who said

P.K. gives a speech during a press conference in celebration of the first anniversary of his donation to the Montreal Children's Hospital, September 2016.

P.K. was "an example of how professional athletes can positively change lives in their communities."

During his time in Nashville, P.K. introduced a program called Blueline Buddies. The program brought together members of the Metro Nashville Police Department and underprivileged kids. Whenever the Predators played a home game, P.K. purchased tickets and arranged for a police officer and a child from an inner-city community to go to dinner before the game and watch the game. P.K. met with them before and after he played to give them a special night to look forward to. He also made Christmas time special in Nashville with his Subban Sleigh day. Children who were ill with sickle cell disease (which affects mostly people of colour) went on a sleigh ride through the city and then P.K. threw a party for them at the Predators' Bridgestone Arena.

P.K. has said that he feels athletes should serve as role models in their communities. On May 2, 2018, P.K. was named one of the three finalists for the King Clancy Memorial Trophy. The trophy goes to a player who best demonstrates leadership qualities, on and off the ice, while giving back to his community.

P.K. has a strong commitment to those feeling overwhelmed by racism and hatred. He makes a point of trying to break down barriers and stand up against racism. P.K. knows the pain that racism causes and he reaches out to connect with kids who are experiencing it.

Two disturbing instances of racism came to P.K.'s attention in 2019. One involved 13-year-old Divyne Apollon II who played for the Metro Maple Leafs in Odenton, Maryland. After reading how Divyne faced monkey sounds and the N-word from an opposing team at a tournament, P.K. spoke to Divyne and his dad on the phone. He offered words of encouragement to the young player.

P.K. also sent a video text message to 13-year-old Ty Cornett, who was being called racist names while playing hockey. "I can tell you this right now — as long as you're still breathing in this world, you got to believe in yourself and let nobody tell you what you can and can't do, especially if it's because of the colour of your skin," P.K. said in the video. "In this world, some things happen that we don't really understand. That's okay. We don't have to understand them. All we need to do is understand ourselves, believe in ourselves, keep trying and keep pushing forward. I just want to tell you that when you're playing hockey, you play because you love the game and you want to play. Let nobody take that away from you."

P.K. also looks to the past, and never forgets to recognize those who came before him who worked toward social justice. When the announcement was made in 2018 that Willie O'Ree, the NHL's first black player, was to be inducted into the Hockey Hall of Fame, P.K. posted a video of congratulations on Twitter. He thanked O'Ree for being an inspiration to players of colour.

In an ESPN interview, P.K. said, "I never look at myself as a black player. I think of myself as a hockey player who wants to be the best hockey player in the league. I know I'm black. Everyone knows I'm black. But I don't want to be defined as a black hockey player. I want to be defined as one of the best hockey players. Or the best hockey player."

On his website, P.K. has a statement that reads, "I'm more than just a hockey player." In the ESPN interview, he talked about wanting to "transcend the game." In addition to his talent as an athlete, his charity work and his many business projects, P.K. may have an eye on life in the media too. He has appeared on the TV shows *Just for Laughs* and *The Daily Show* with Trevor Noah. He's been on a number of sports anchor desks doing commentary. He even hosted his own show for NBCsports.com for which he interviewed NHL stars and celebrities.

As the world of pro hockey keeps

Willie O'Ree, shown here in 2018, was the first black player in the NHL.

Willie O'Ree

Willie O'Ree was a black Canadian hockey player born in Fredericton, New Brunswick in 1935. When O'Ree played his first NHL game on January 16, 1958, with the Boston Bruins, it was the first time a black player had ever played in the NHL. Willie was blind in one eye, but he never let it slow him down. Later Willie took on the role as the NHL's Diversity Ambassador, sharing the message that hockey is for everyone!

growing and changing, so does the world of P.K. Subban. In July 2019 it was announced that P.K. had been traded to the New Jersey Devils. In true P.K. style, he posted a video about his excitement at joining the team. In the video, P.K. jumps into a swimming pool on July 4th, Independence Day in the US, wearing an American flag bikini! A few days later he invited fans to "Hit Me Up!" on Instagram, posting his personal phone number and inviting people to give him a call.

In an interview with Sean Fitz-Gerald back in 2014, the *National Post* reporter asked P.K. to finish this sentence: "By the time I'm done . . ." P.K. finished the sentence with "the world will know my name. Boom!" and flashed his great big smile at the reporter. Today everyone knows who he is. Even better, everyone knows the character and compassion he learned from his family and carried on through his life.

P.K. Subban Career Highlights

OHL First All-Star Team 2009

AHL All-Rookie Team 2010

AHL First All-Star Team 2010

AHL All-Rookie Team 2011

President's Award 2009–10

James Norris Memorial Trophy 2013

NHL First All-Star Team 2013, 2015

Meritorious Service Cross, Governor General of Canada 2016

Played in NHL All-Star Game 2016, 2017

NHL All-Star Game Team Captain 2018, 2019

Glossary

A, AA, AAA: The three competitive levels in minor hockey.

Artifact: A man-made item that has some form of cultural interest.

Billet: To offer the use of a private family home for a player or student to live in temporarily while playing or studying away from home.

Blue line: The lines painted on the ice dividing centre ice (the neutral zone) from the attacking or defending zones.

Conference Divisions: The National Hockey League is made up of 31 hockey teams. The league divides these teams into conferences, the Eastern Conference and the Western Conference. Each conference is subdivided into two more divisions. This helps the league manage the teams' playing schedule by dividing the season up into different divisions.

Defencemen: The two players who play in front of the goalie to help keep the opposing team from getting shots on the net.

Draft: A selection process of choosing players to become members of a sports team.

GTHL/Greater Toronto Hockey League/"the G": The largest minor ice hockey league in the world.

Hashtag: A hash or pound sign followed by a word or phrase run together, used on social media to identify a particular topic.

Hat trick: When a player scores three goals during a game.

House league/Local League: A recreational level of play. House league players are almost always given equal ice time regardless of skill or talent, and house league teams play in fewer tournaments throughout the season.

Lockout: A time when owners stop players from coming to work on their teams. The owners do not pay the players and there are no hockey games played.

Off-season: The time of year when players are not playing.

Overtime: Time played after the regular period of play has run out.

Power Play: When one or more players from a team is in the penalty box and the other team has the advantage of more players on the ice.

Proverb: A traditional saying that simplifies the truth by using common examples.

Racism: A belief or way of thinking that discriminates against people who have different skin colour or ethnicity.

Represent: To act or speak for someone.

Rookie: A player in their first year.

Slapshot: The most powerful shot in hockey. The player takes a hard swing at the puck with the blade of their stick.

Stanley Cup: The trophy awarded at the end of the NHL playoff season to the championship team.

Veteran: A player who has played for a long time.

Warm-up: Preparing the body for physical performance.

Acknowledgements

An incredible team of supporters came together to help me write this book.

Writing can be a lonely process sometimes, but I always felt I had a full roster of teammates helping me reach my goal. P.K. Subban's story is one that needs to be shared and I want to thank the following people for their efforts in bringing it to these pages.

Many thanks go to my publishers, James Lorimer and Carrie Gleason for embracing the concept of this book from the beginning. I am truly thankful for the assistance of the talented staff at James Lorimer & Company.

Much gratitude goes to my editor Kat Mototsune for her never-ending support, direction, friendship and hockey knowledge!

I am indebted to the following people

who offered their stories, history and knowledge of hockey to help tell P.K.'s story: Runnymede C.I. former staff and students, Christopher Tranter, Sophie Giorno, Hugh Rowland, Carlotta Lovell; Izak Westgate and the Hockey Hall of Fame; Valerie Frost — The Montreal Children's Hospital, Dean Lisk — *The Toronto Star*; Bill Hamade; Mark Mah; Carl Weekes; George Stavro and the Etobicoke Hockey League; Randy Jacobs and the Markham Islanders, (GTHL) Greater Toronto Hockey League; Gord Simmonds, George Burnett, Aaron Bell; Belleville Bulls; Peggy Chapman, Dan Bushey, Derek Wills — Sportsnet 960 *The FAN.*

Unfortunately, I was unable to interview P.K. Subban for this book, but I had the great fortune of being able to research his life through the incredible media outlets that report on sports in North

America. I am very appreciative of the following media organizations who covered P.K.'s story on and off the ice: NHL.com/canadiens, sportsnet.ca, montrealgazette.com, NHL.com, tsn.ca, cbc.ca, thehockeynews.com, colorofhockey.com, ESPN.com, ontariohockeyleague.com, *National Post*, *The New Yorker*, *Sports Illustrated*, thecanadianencyclopedia.ca, *Toronto Life*, *Toronto Star* and the Hockey Hall of Fame.

All this wouldn't be possible if it were not for my home team — my family.

George, Matthew, Nella, Jude and Desmond (Desi) — hockey fans, book lovers and the characters that make my story special.

I will be forever grateful for the support of my friends and colleagues at the Toronto Public Library, especially Vann-Ly Cheng and Doriana Onorati. A special thank you goes to the members of my Number 9 Writers' Group for their inspiring support.

A gracious thank you goes to the Subban family who have shared their inspiring family history with us all. And finally to P.K. who not only chased his dream but watches over those who are reaching for the stars too. You are truly more than just a hockey player.

Photo Credits

Aaron Bell: p. 49, p. 51, p. 65, p. 68, p. 115

Bill Hamade: p. 96, p. 97

Carlotta Lovell: p. 45

Courtesy of countryflags.com: p. 14

Courtesy of *The Toronto Star*: p. 21

George Stavro and the Etobicoke Hockey League: p. 29

Jude Rondina: p. 73, p. 99

Matthew Manor and the Hockey Fall of Fame: p. 129

Peggy Chapman: p. 56, p. 58

Randy Jacobs: p. 43

Rebl House: p. 124

Richard Bartlaga: p. 26

Index